After the Funeral

by
Jane Loretta Winsch

illustrated by
Pam Keating

PAULIST PRESS
New York and Mahwah, N.J.

Library of Congress Cataloging-in-Publication Data

Winsch, Jane Loretta.
    After the funeral / by Jane Loretta Winsch ; illustrated
by Pam Keating.
        p.   cm.
    Summary: Discusses the various feelings accompanying
the death of a loved one, including sadness, grief, and the
fear of death itself.
    ISBN 0-8091-6625-9 (alk. paper)
    1. Bereavement in children.   2. Grief in children.
3. Death—Psychological aspects—Juvenile literature.
[1. Death. 2. Grief.]   I. Keating, Pamela T., ill.   II. Title.
BF723.G75W547   1995
155.9′37′083—dc20   95-5574
                                                                  CIP
                                                                   AC

Published by Paulist Press
997 Macarthur Boulevard
Mahwah, New Jersey 07430

Printed and bound in the
United States of America

The bereaved children I've had the privilege of working with "gave" me this book. I thank them for it.

Also, special thanks to my friend and talented illustrator, Pam Keating, for bringing this "seed" to life in so many ways.

I dedicate it to my dearest friends and family, most especially my sister, Fran. By her example, she teaches us all to begin again.

"You'll laugh at me."
"No, I won't."
"Yes you will. It's dumb."

This is a book to help you see that nothing you feel is dumb—even when you think *no one* could ever have felt the way you do.

After the Funeral was written to share with you some of the secret thoughts and experiences other boys and girls have had when someone special has died.

But he learned that he didn't have to be afraid of being left alone.

"Daddy promised there would always be

someone to love and care

Even though Maureen's daddy has died,
she keeps waiting for him to
walk through the front door
at 6:00—

like always.

"But you know—Mom does too.
    She told me that facing what death
    has done takes time—
    even for grown-ups."

After the death of his sister,
Patrick had a secret:
"Sometimes I hug Jeanie's sweatshirt.

I even put it on.

Still.

It always makes me feel closer to her."

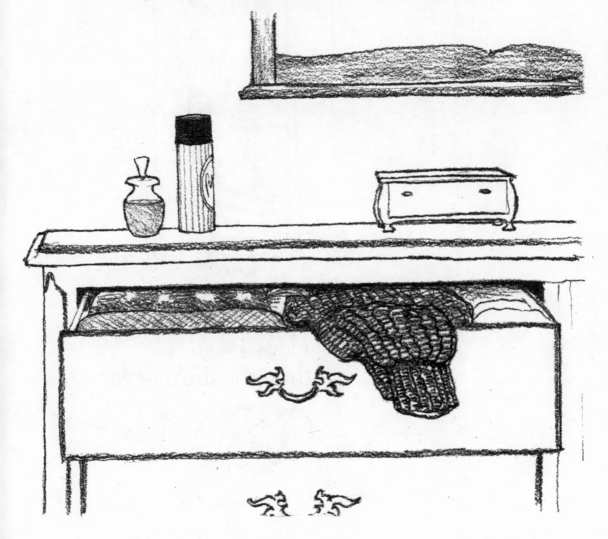

After his father died,
Robbie was sad
because his mom cried
and cried.

"I thought she'd never

be happy again.

But you know—just like me—

Mommy needs time—
    she misses Daddy too."

At their baby sister's funeral,
Darren wondered how his big brother
kept from crying—
when he
couldn't stop.

"But now I've learned that everyone
               handles sadness
               in their own way."

It made Maria sad that
her classmates never said a word
about her Grandma's death.

"It was like it never happened.

But they really did know—
and care.
They just didn't know what to say."

It was hard for Peter to concentrate on school work after his mom's funeral.

Matt tried
to hold all his feelings inside
when his best friend died.

Makeba was scared of her Grandpa's house—

"...because that's where he died.

But you know, when I was ready,
Daddy took my hand,
and we walked in there
together."

Eddie didn't want to go
into his brother's room:

"It made me miss him even more.

But I knew that one day I'd be ready
to walk through that door."

"I hear Daddy's voice in my heart,
but I wish I could hear him in my ears.
I just wish I could see him again."

"You will see him again, Billy.
My Grandma says that God offers all of us
eternal life and we will meet again
one day in
heaven."

"Every religious tradition offers us hope that we will have a life that goes beyond our life on this earth."

One more secret—If you keep your
special person in your heart and in your
prayers they'll always be part of you.